IMAGES OF ENG

Shirebrook
A Second Selection

A future star. Charlie Wall (left, in scout uniform) pictured with his father and sister Enid (standing, right) some time during the 1930s. A talented trumpeter who began his musical career with the Shirebrook Salvation Army band, Charlie later played in the dance bands of Billy Ternent and Bill Petters, and led his own band for eighteen years in Aberdeen.

IMAGES OF ENGLAND

Shirebrook
A Second Selection

Geoff Sadler

NONSUCH

Early Bath. A very young Dennis Middleton enjoys a bath outside the family home at 8 Church Drive, Model Village, some time during the late 1930s. His mother, Mrs Phyllis Middleton, lends a hand.

First published 1995
This new pocket edition 2006
Images unchanged from first edition

Nonsuch Publishing Limited
The Mill, Brimscombe Port,
Stroud, Gloucestershire, GL5 2QG
www.nonsuch-publishing.com

Nonsuch Publishing is an imprint of Tempus Publishing Group

British Library Cataloguing in Publication Data.
A catalogue record for this book is available from the British Library.

ISBN 1-84588-318-7

Typesetting and origination by Nonsuch Publishing Limited
Printed in Great Britain by Oaklands Book Services Limited

Contents

Acknowledgements

Sincere and grateful thanks are due to everyone who has helped and encouraged me in compiling this book. In particular I would like to express my gratitude to Mrs Joan Watts for her generous gift of sixteen excellent old photographs of Shirebrook, previously unseen by the author; to Mrs Jessie Kay for the loan of some fascinating historical material on Kay's business and the local Nursing Association; to Mrs Helena Lyons for photographs of the well-known footballing Lyons family; to Malcolm Shaw for further items from his own collection and that of his late father Henry Shaw; to Mr and Mrs Burrows and the Old Warsop Society, and to Mr William Eaton for late and welcome additions to the book, and to my good friend Ernest Roberts, his wife, Emma, and his brothers, John and Kenneth Roberts, for numerous interesting shots from their family album.

Sincere thanks also to the following, for their kind permission to reproduce the photographs here: Mrs H. Barke, Mr D. Bener, Mr S. Bettison, Mr G. Bradbury, Mr R. Bulloch, Mr J. Collier, Mr F. Cooke, Mr G. Cox, Mr W. Dodds, Mr & Mrs Foottit, Mr J.S. Fowler, Mr C.J. French, Mrs Hartshorne, Mrs G. Kettle, Mr J. Middleton, Mr J. Mitchell, Mr D. Neale, Mrs Nuttall, Mr J. Price, Mrs Randle, Mrs E. Redfern, Mr R. Scruby, Mr H. Tarrant, Mr J. Tomlinson, Mrs N. Watkinson.

Thanks also to Mr Jeremy Plews, Mr Roger Grayson and Mansfield 'Chad'; Mr K. Beeston and British Coal Corporation; Shirebrook Ex-Servicemen's Club.

For information and advice, thanks to Mr D. Bilzon, Mr D. Crute (Mansfield Local Studies Library), Mrs K. Hill, Mr M. Jobling (Ilkeston Library), Mr L. Little, Sub-Officer Eric Lomax and Shirebrook Fire Brigade, Mr M. Newham, Mr P. Pawson, Mr Duncan Payne (Ilkeston F.C. historian), Mr E. Smith, Mr Tony Warriner, Mr Dennis Webster and Shirebrook Town Council.

Thanks to Shirebrook & District Local History Group, whose members as always provided valuable information and support.

Finally, if anyone whose name should appear here has been inadvertently omitted, please accept my sincere apologies, and rest assured that your contribution is greatly appreciated.

Kettle Brothers on site. Members of the Shirebrook firm of Kettle Brothers, their haulage vehicle in the background, examine an unidentified building site in this shot from the 1920s. Patrick Kettle is the man shown third from left. The firm freighted bricks and building supplies to sites all over the country, and George Kettle's garage is still in operation on Langwith Road.

Introduction

Welcome to *Shirebrook: a Second Selection*, the second study of Shirebrook in words and pictures in this series. I was delighted to accept Chalford Publishing's kind invitation to produce this book so soon after the first, in spite of the hard work involved. To begin with, Chalford *asked* me, and as one whose time as a writer is usually spent persuading publishers to accept my work, it's always a pleasant surprise to produce one at the publisher's request. Better still, I was asked following publication of the first book, so I have the pleasure of knowing that one has sold well and that success is expected for the second, which surely suggests we must be doing something right!

    Most important of all, however, is the feeling I have that such an opportunity may not come again, if ever. There has to be a limit to the number of photographs available, and therefore to the books that can be written on the subject. Eventually, the seemingly endless flow of pictures must become exhausted? On the other hand, I've been proved wrong so often on this score, I'd be more than pleased to be mistaken yet again.

Since the first book came out, Shirebrook has undergone a number of drastic changes, most of them unwelcome. The closure of the colliery last year ended almost a century of its history as a mining village, brutally destroying its industrial base. We have seen the conseqences in widespread unemployment, the cutting back of business, and the rundown of residential areas so long geared to a thriving pit. A visible rise in crime, and an apparent lack of resources to combat this and other problems, have led in many places to a feeling of abandonment and insecurity. Efforts are being made to improve the situation, for which our local leaders are to be commended, but the future for Shirebrook remains uncertain. Further change is coming, we may be sure. But will it be for the better?

To my mind, this makes the compiling of this book even more important. Only by exploring and understanding our past can we come to terms with what lies ahead, and establish a base for further progress. This doesn't mean that we have to don a pair of rose-tinted spectacles and bathe in nostalgia; then, as nowadays, life had plenty of unpleasant aspects. The 1926 Strike, the Depression of the 1930s, and the horrors of two World Wars, are the obvious examples. And few of us, I suspect, would really like to return to the dubious standards of health and hygiene that prevailed in the early decades of this century. This negative side was balanced by the many positive qualities of those years – the strong sense of community and comradeship, the patriotism and civic pride, and the fighting spirit that overcame the worst of obstacles placed in its path. To truly understand the past is to be aware of its mistakes and strive to avoid them, while doing our best to retain and build on the many achievements and successes. If we are able to do this, then we can surely look forward to a more hopeful future.

Shirebrook: a Second Selection shows the life of our village in all its aspects, from the 1890s to the 1990s, and from studio portraits to family snaps. I hope you will read, view and enjoy what it has to offer, because that is why it was first put together; but perhaps it won't end there. I have learned a great deal while studying these photographs. Maybe, after reading this, some of you may also feel that you have discovered something you didn't know before.

Geoff Sadler
1995

One

Around the Village

Rock Cottages, Main Street. Possibly some of the earliest buildings to be erected in Shirebrook, these stone cottages dated back to the eighteenth century, and were a feature of the old, agricultural village. Adjoining the main east-to-west thoroughfare leading into Shirebrook, they continued in existence until their eventual demolition in the 1960s.

Gate Inn, King Edward Street. A striking view of Shirebrook's oldest working public house, which is known to have operated from the late eighteenth century. At one time the main road did not extend beyond the inn, access being obtained by a gate – from which the hostelry takes its name – to an unmade footpath. King Edward Street, built in the 1900s and clearly visible on the left, establishes the time as our own century, possibly around 1910.

Mrs Ada Shipley. A picture taken outside her home on Portland Road in the 1950s. The tall building in the background is the Station Hotel, which like several of the houses on Portland Road was originally built in the late 1890s.

Mrs Chadbourne and family. A portrait from around 1900. The Chadbournes lived at Sookholme Farm, a short distance south-east of the village.

Ward's Corner, King Edward Street. Leonard Ward established his confectionery business at No. 2 King Edward Street in the early 1920s, and the site of his premises at the junction of King Edward Street and Victoria Street became popularly known as Ward's Corner. After many years of service the business changed hands, and has currently ceased operations, but was a thriving concern when this shot was taken in the 1930s.

Stanley family and friends, 1930s. A group photograph taken on the slope behind the family shop on Station Road. Back row (left to right): Irene Stanley; Vic Stanley; Mrs Stanley; Mrs Williamson. Front row (left to right): Doreen Stanley; Mr S. Zelickman, Sr.; Rita Pickering; Marjorie Stanley, Mrs Pickering.

St Joseph's Church under construction. Situated on Langwith Road to the east of Shirebrook, St Joseph's Chuch was built to accommodate the village's Roman Catholic worshippers, and was opened in 1908. It has associations with Father Rex Hattersley, whose son later became a noted politician and author. Here, workers pose with the church still in the process of construction behind them, some time during the year 1907.

Young man at home. A youthful Graham Shaw, pictured outside his home at Hillcrest, during the 1960s. The building of Hillcrest was part of a series of housing developments which took place on the western side of Shirebrook prior to the Second World War.

R. Furniss & Son, Station Road. The Furniss brothers were in business as butchers in Shirebrook from the late nineteenth century, and appear in directories for the 1890s with premises on both Main Street and Station Road. Here, in what appears to be a pre-war shot, a member of the family firm stands in the doorway of the Station Road establishment in the centre of an unidentified group of relatives or passers-by.

A.E. Hartshorne, Station Road. Mary Hartshorne's drapery business was established on Langwith Road by the early 1930s, and continued into the war years. The business later moved its premises to Station Road, opposite the Beehive Stores, where this picture was taken in the 1950s. The shop was closed a few years later.

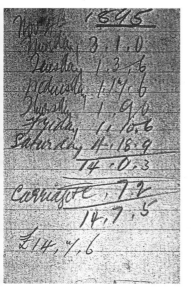

A historic account. Pages from an account book dating back to 1895, which was kept by S.H. Kay on behalf of Andrew Derbyshire, outfitter, of Main Street. Mr Kay later purchased the business from Mr Derbyshire (his uncle) and it remained a family concern for over 70 years.

Kay's Advertisement, 1934. Taken from a fundraising publication by the Shirebrook & District Nursing Association, of which Mrs J. Kay was a founder member. A thriving and popular business employing five staff, Kay's served the Shirebrook public almost three-quarters of a century.

Marshall's Advertisement, 1934. Another advert from the same publication. George Marshall's printing firm was already operating from its premises on Main Street as early as 1908, and continued into the post-war period. Marshall was the printer of Shirebrook's Coronation Handbook and Souvenir of 1937, and this advertisement is a good example of his lively, illustrative style.

Jams and Sweetmeats.

LEMON CHEESE.

One lb. Loaf Sugar, 4 Eggs, 3 Lemons, 2 ozs. fresh Butter. Take the yolks of 4 and the whites of 3 eggs, add to them the grated rind of 3 lemons and the juice of 2 (be careful to remove all pips). Melt the butter, add all the contents and bring to a boil on a slow fire.

—Mrs. R. Ayres, Langwith Junction.

APPLE AND MARROW CHUTNEY.

Two lbs. Marrow, 1 lb. Apples, ½-lb. Onions, 1 pt. Vinegar, ½-lb. Loaf Sugar, 2 ozs. Ginger (bruised), a few Chillies and Peppercorns, ½-oz. Turmeric, 1 tablespoonful Cornflour. Peel and cut the marrow into small chunks, sprinkle with salt and let it stand for 24 hours. Strain and add chopped onions, apples, sugar and vinegar. Put spices into a muslin bag and boil all for 1 hour. Mix turmeric and cornflour into paste with a little vinegar and boil for 5 or 10 minutes, stirring all the time.

—Mrs. H. White, Shirebrook.

GOOSEBERRY JAM.

Boil 1 lb. Gooseberries in 1 pint Water for ½-hour. Add 2 lbs. Sugar, boil another ½-hour and put into jars.

—Mrs. Willson, Shirebrook.

LEMON CURD.

Four ozs. Butter, 1 lb. Sugar, 4 small Lemons, 4 Eggs. Beat the eggs, add sugar and butter, grated rind of lemon and juice. Put in double pan and stir with wooden spoon until the mixture is as thick as honey.

—Mrs. Carl Nicholson, Shirebrook.

EVERTON TOFFEE.

Nine ozs. Butter, 1½ lbs. Loaf Sugar, ½-cup Water, ½-teaspoonful Cream of Tartar. Boil for 20 minutes stirring all the time.

—Mrs. E. Knighton, Shirebrook.

MARROW CREAM.

Two lbs. Marrow, 2 lbs. Loaf Sugar, 4 Lemons, 4 ozs. Butter. Boil marrow until tender, drain until it ceases to drop, beat it to paste, put into pan again with sugar, butter, rind and juice of lemons, and boil until it makes a nice smooth paste.

—Mrs. J. Parker, Shirebrook.

DELICIOUS APPLE JAM which will keep for years.

Weigh equal quantities of Brown Sugar and good sour Apples. Pare, core, and chop apples fine. Make a good, clear syrup of the sugar, add apples, juice and grated rind of 3 lemons, and a few pieces of white Ginger. Boil until the apple looks clear and yellow. On no account forget the ginger.

—Mrs. Bradbury, Shirebrook.

ECONOMICAL MARMALADE.

One lb. Marmalade Oranges, 1 Lemon, 6 lbs. Sugar, 9 tumblers cold Water. Cut the fruit into 8 lengthwise and take out the pips. Slice as thinly as possible through both skin and pulp. Put in large pan and set aside for 24 hours covered with cold water. When ready, boil in pan for 1 hour or until the skins are tender, keeping the water made up to the original quantity as it boils away. Set aside until cold then add the sugar. Boil again and remove scum. In about ½-hour it should jelly. Seal down whilst hot.

—Mrs. Squires, Shirebrook.

Some Shirebrook recipes. A sample page from the 1934 booklet, showing a few of the recipes provided by local people. Several well-known Shirebrook names are included, among them Mrs Carl Nicholson.

Market Hotel and Market Place, 1920s. Opened in 1907, the Market Hotel is popularly known as the 'Drum', and is here being viewed from the far, Victoria Street, side of the Market Place. The gentleman in the foreground is the late Frederick French, Sr.

Main Street and Central Drive, 1960s. Mrs Madge Davies (née Flint), with daughter Lindy and friend, taking a walk along Main Street towards the centre of the village. Behind them on the left Central Drive leads uphill to the Model Village, while further back Main Street itself negotiates a bend beneath the old Great Northern Railway Bridge – demolished in the 1970s.

As far as the eye can see. An interesting view from Warren Terrace, on the western side of the village, probably taken during the 1960s. In the foreground is the farmhouse and outbuildings owned by the Reddish family, and behind it on the far left is Rockleigh Houses, once the family residence. Both have now disappeared, with modern buildings occupying the site. On the right of the picture is 'Thorneycroft', which has for some years been the home of Miss Jessie Reddish. Between the buildings Main Street (or Warren Terrace) leads down to the village centre, passing under the Great Northern Railway bridge with its raised embankment, also long since vanished. Beyond the bridge the parish church of Holy Trinity appears on the right, while in the distance on the left are the headgear and chimney of Warsop Main Colliery, which closed a few years ago

Holy Cross Church, Upper Langwith. Upper Langwith is a small rural settlement which adjoins Shirebrook on its north-eastern side. The original stone church was known as St Helen's in its early days, becoming the Church of the Holy Cross in the late nineteenth century. It was restored and extended in 1878, the chancel being rebuilt and enlarged, and addition made to the nave. The photograph, probably from around 1920, reflects the rustic charm of church and village alike.

Poulter Street, Langwith. A view along the main street of Langwith village, again probably dating from the 1920s. The largest of the five settlements collectively known as Langwith, the village is situated on the eastern edge of Derbyshire, close to the Nottinghamshire border. The tree stump on the right has now disappeared, but Harrison's Portland Garage continued into modern times. The colliery, whose chimney appears in the background, closed in the 1970s.

Tea Party, Pentecostal Mission. Built around 1950, the Mission on Manvers Street replaced a much earlier building on the same site. Shown here at this 1950s party are (left to right): Alan Warriner; -?-; Derek Parker; -?-; -?-; -?-; Derek Edmunds (with lifted cup); ? Fritchley; Leonard Edmunds; Mr Gunton (standing); 'Duke' Howarth (at head of table); ? Larbey ?; Harry Roberts; John Saunderson; Dougie Saunderson; Willie Gunton; and John Roberts.

A vanished street. Cavendish Street corner, at its junction with Station Road, in the late 1960s. Cavendish Street was one of several streets leading off Station Road, and close to the Market Place, which were originally driven through rows of existing buildings to provide access after 1910 and eventually demolished in the early 1970s. The young girl in the shot is Susan Kelly.

Moorley's, Station Road. A view of the tobacconist's shop owned by Frederick Moorley, at the junction of Station Road with Morris Street, probably taken shortly before the First World War. The walls and windows are crammed with advertisements, the familiar names of St Bruno and Player's Navy Cut jostling for position with the more esoteric brands of Mitchell's 'Tam o' Shanter' and Simon's 'Evergreen', while the posters by the door announce nightly performances of *Her Dreadful Secret* at the Town Hall, Main Street (owned by Thomas Moorley, a relative of the proprietor). In the foreground a young child rides in a makeshift carriage along Station Road, whose unmade surface betrays evidence of horse-drawn transport having passed this way.

A night at the Northern. Four Shirebrook residents enjoy a quiet pint at the Great Northern Hotel on Main Street. The man on the far left is unidentified, but the others (left to right) are: Leo Lefley, Bob Bulloch, and his father, Mr Bulloch.

The Road to Warsop Main. Another shot from the 1960s showing the well-travelled footpath which passed the boundary bridge on its way out of Shirebrook to Warsop Main Colliery in Nottinghamshire. Many local miners worked at Warsop, and took this route to the pit every morning. The colliery headstocks, now destroyed, may be seen in the distance.

Empire Theatre, Station Road. Established as a theatre in 1910, the Empire was built by the local firm of F.H. & J.W. Moore to the design of architect Frederick Hopkinson. Its electrically-lit public hall provided seating for 1000 and was notable for its large (30ft by 53ft) stage. Owned by Thomas Moorley, who also ran the Town Hall theatre and held the licence for the Great Northern Hotel, the Empire became a local landmark, and one of the main venues for Shirebrook entertainment under booking manager Henry W. Ruggins. This shot from its early, halcyon days reveals the distinctive structure with its arches and the wrought iron grille above the entrance. In later years it was transformed into a cinema, re-opening in 1952 as part of the Regal Group, and is currently in use as a bingo hall.

Live tonight. One of the many groups of entertainers booked by H.W. Ruggins for performances at the Empire prior to the First World War.

Stanleys', Station Road. John Stanley takes a well earned rest in front of the family shop at 144 Station Road in this prewar 1930s photograph. The Stanleys' wireless dealing business had been founded by Mrs Harriet Stanley early in the same decade.

On 'Empire Corner'. John Stanley and his neighbour, Mr Zelickman, Jr., on open ground to the rear of their shops on Station Road, at what was then known as 'Empire Corner'. Zelickman's furniture shop at 132 Station Road was only a short distance from Mr Stanley's premises, and both businesses were active in the 1930s and '40s. The building directly behind them is the slaughterhouse of the butcher Joseph Parker.

Jug and Glass, Nether Langwith. A group of locals (with attendant dog) gather to face the camera outside Nether Langwith's well-known hostelry. An attractive rural village, Nether Langwith lies just across the border into Nottinghamshire, but is recognizably a part of the Langwith group of settlements. The Jug and Glass is a favoured location for both locals and visitors. The sign above the door, showing Frank Willis as licensee, suggests a date between 1912 and 1920.

Stuffynwood Hall. Situated to the south of the village, Stuffynwood Hall was built in 1858 on a site previously occupied by Robert Malkin, and for forty years was the home of the local squire, Joseph Paget, who presided over the life of the farming village. His death in 1896, the year the colliery was sunk, signalled the end of an era, and after brief occupation by the M.P. Arthur B. Markham, the Hall was allowed to deteriorate and is now a ruin.

Two

Birth and Death of a Colliery

Early days. Shirebrook Colliery shortly after construction in the 1890s. The pit was sunk by Shirebrook Colliery Co. Ltd. (Managing Director Professor Arnold Lupton) in 1896, and its founding brought a massive influx of workers to the village, the population increasing tenfold within five years. Here the original wooden headstocks and tall colliery chimney are shown, features which dominated the village skyline for years to come.

Under construction. An earlier shot from c. 1896–97, showing extensive fencing and scaffolding around the as yet unfinished colliery buildings.

Headstocks with conveyor. A second view of the wooden headstocks, this time with the coal conveyor and its wooden gantry clearly shown on the left of the picture.

Red Bridge, with lady. The 'Red Bridge', at the junction of Wood Lane and Sookholme Road, spanned the railway lines and their regular coal freight deliveries, and was a well-known local landmark. The lady's identity remains a mystery, but the advertisement on the bridge itself reads: 'Shirebrook Colliery – Best Coal – Steam-Furnace-House.'

Pit Horses and Drivers. A group of animals and their handlers in the pit yard. This picture was taken at the turn of the century, but pit ponies and horses were used in Shirebrook Colliery until modern times, the last ponies being led out in 1971.

Shirebrook No. 2 Colliery Rescue Team. One of three rescue teams active in the colliery during its early years. Like most other pits, Shirebrook had its share of serious accidents, and the work of its rescue teams demanded brave, dedicated men. Apart from the uniformed superintendent, Mr J.G. Huskisson, none of this team has been identified, but the photograph certainly dates from before 1929.

Rescue Team, c. 1950. The hut which later served as the old colliery offices is on the left of the picture. Among those shown here are Harry Roberts, safety representative (back row, far left) and to his right Shadrach Randall, John Oxley, Joe Platts, Jack Hall. The middle row are unidentified, but in the front row are F. Kyte (second left), J. Hall and Cyril Burden.

5. No notice to terminate contracts, and no strike, cessation of work, or alterations in the working conditions on either side shall take place at any Colliery where negotiations are pending, and until the question or questions in dispute have been brought before and fully considered by the respective Associations.

6. The Committee and Board shall be elected by the respective Associations.

7. The Owners' and Deputies' Associations shall each elect a Secretary, who shall be empowered to record the proceedings of the Board, and the Minutes shall be agreed upon between the Secretaries prior to being placed before the meeting next following for approval.

8. Any or all questions to be referred by the Committee to the Board for settlement shall be stated in writing and signed by representatives of both Associations clearly setting out the nature of the question or dispute at issue, and such statement shall be lodged with the Secretaries to the Board at least seven days prior to the date when the meeting is to be held.

The Board shall meet within thirty days from the date of such reference.

Either side shall be at liberty to make any counter claim or proposal, to be lodged with the respective Secretaries within seven days of the receipt of the original claim.

9. On any case being submitted to the Board the parties may bring forward any necessary evidence, but the Board shall have power to stop or disallow such evidence as it may consider to be out of order.

If the number of members present representing the Owners and Deputies respectively is unequal, the voting shall be deemed to be equal if all the Deputies' Representatives present vote one way and those of the Owners the other.

10. All expenses incurred by the Board (other than the expenses of the Representatives) shall be borne equally by the Owners' and Deputies' Associations.

11. Cases shall not be reconsidered until after a lapse of six months from the date of an agreement affecting the question proposed to be dealt with in the case.

12. Six months' notice shall be given on either side of the intention to terminate this Agreement.

2

AGREEMENT made between the Midland Counties Colliery Owners' Association and the National Association of Colliery Owners' Deputies with regard to payment of Wages and conditions of work applicable to Deputies employed in the Counties of Nottingham and Derby being Members of the last mentioned Association.

1. WAGE.

A Minimum Basis Wage of Nine Shillings and Sixpence (9/6) per day, plus 23 and One-third per cent. and War Bonus and War Wage.

The above to be subject to advances and reductions as awarded by the Conciliation Board, and Controller.

No reduction to be made in cases of Deputies now paid above this rate, and conditions with regard to extra time to be left as at present with the different Companies to make their own arrangements.

Facilities to be given for Deputies to work six days per week, or to be paid six day's wage.

2. OVERTIME.

Overtime to be paid for at the above rate. No count to be made for Overtime when Deputies are detained short periods after their ordinary shift owing to unforeseen circumstances.

3. SICKNESS.

When a Deputy is medically unfit to attend his employment, half-pay to be allowed during the first four weeks, and quarter-pay during the next eight weeks, War Wage not included. This allowance to be the amount allowed per annum.

The definition of this Clause to be that the allowance of time granted to a Deputy when off sick to be calculated on the year, that is the year to date from the date of this agreement.

3

A page from the handbook of the National Association of Colliery Deputies, showing agreements in operation from 12 September 1924.

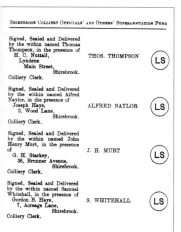

SHIREBROOK COLLIERY OFFICIALS' AND OTHERS' SUPERANNUATION FUND

Signed, Sealed and Delivered by the within named Thomas Thompson, in the presence of
H. C. Nuttall,
  Lyndene,
    Main Street,
      Shirebrook,
Colliery Clerk.

THOS. THOMPSON   (LS)

Signed, Sealed and Delivered by the within named Alfred Naylor, in the presence of
Joseph Hays,
  3, Wood Lane,
    Shirebrook,
Colliery Clerk.

ALFRED NAYLOR   (LS)

Signed, Sealed and Delivered by the within named John Henry Murt, in the presence of
G. H. Starkey,
  38, Brunner Avenue,
    Shirebrook,
Colliery Clerk.

J. H. MURT   (LS)

Signed, Sealed and Delivered by the within named Samuel Whitehall, in the presence of
Gordon B. Hays,
  7, Acreage Lane,
    Shirebrook,
Colliery Clerk.

S. WHITEHALL   (LS)

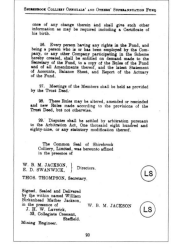

SHIREBROOK COLLIERY OFFICIALS' AND OTHERS' SUPERANNUATION FUND

once of any change therein and shall give such other information as may be required including a Certificate of his birth.

26. Every person having any rights in the Fund, and being a person who is or has been employed by the Company, or any other Company participating in the Scheme hereby created, shall be entitled on demand made to the Secretary of the Fund, to a copy of the Rules of the Fund and of all Amendments thereof, and the latest Statement of Accounts, Balance Sheet, and Report of the Actuary of the Fund.

27. Meetings of the Members shall be held as provided by the Trust Deed.

28. These Rules may be altered, amended or rescinded and new Rules made according to the provisions of the Trust Deed, but not otherwise.

29. Disputes shall be settled by arbitration pursuant to the Arbitration Act, One thousand eight hundred and eighty-nine, or any statutory modification thereof.

The Common Seal of Shirebrook Colliery, Limited, was hereunto affixed in the presence of

W. B. M. JACKSON, } Directors.
E. D. SWANWICK,   }

THOS. THOMPSON, Secretary.   (LS)

Signed, Sealed and Delivered by the within named William Birkenhead Mather Jackson, in the presence of
J. H. W. Laverick,
  22, Collegiate Crescent,
    Sheffield,
Mining Engineer.

W. B. M. JACKSON   (LS)

20

Superannuation Scheme, 1933. A similar page from the Colliery Officials' Superannuation Scheme agreed on 4 March 1933, and showing the signatures of directors and management.

First Aid Competition, 1954. The Shirebrook Colliery Under-21 Team, winners of the Edwinstowe area competition, in the Portland Shield Final. Left to right are: John Roberts, John W. Saunderson, D. Shepherd and Alan Burden. The examiner, with marking board, kneels in the foreground on the right.

Shirebrook Colliery in the 1950s. A photograph by Stanley Bettison showing the complex of colliery buildings, with modern metal headframes and towering chimney. With over half a century of coal production behind it, Shirebrook appeared to be thriving and sure of its future.

Shirebrook Colliery trainees, 1950. Pictured at Crown Farm training centre, with other youngsters from neighbouring collieries in the East Midlands. Among those on view are Jimmy Oxley (front, far left), Bill Hutchinson (third left), Leonard Edmunds (front row, seated fourth left), Cliff Norris (centre, in striped jersey) and John Roberts (seventh from right). To these young men, Shirebrook Colliery's future continuation must have seemed assured. Sadly, it was not to last.

A colliery dies, 1. On Monday 15 August 1994 at 4.00pm, Shirebrook Colliery's No. 1 and No. 2 headstocks were destroyed by controlled explosions. For many, their downfall symbolized the death of the colliery, and with it a way of life that had lasted for close on a century. These pictures were taken by photographer Roger Grayson for the Mansfield 'Chad' newspaper. The Giant Stumbles – the first explosion sets the headstock toppling.

A colliery dies, 2. All the way down ... an eyewitness claims that grown men wept as they watched the headstocks fall.

A colliery dies, 3. To the ground – the heart of a village collapses.

A colliery dies, 4. Annihilation – the felled headgear shatters to fragments in a cloud of dust.

Sole survivor. The N.U.M. office building on the site, soon after the explosions were carried out. The 'Danger of Death' notice seems particularly ironic.

Fragment. The identifying display letter 'S' which crowned the Shirebrook skyline when the pit was in its flourishing prime, now a piece of wreckage in the dust as 98 years of coal-mining are reduced to rubble.

Three

Bodies, Hearts and Minds

A.R.P. Class, Carter Lane. Members of the Saint John Ambulance Brigade muster outside Carter Lane School for an Air Lock Demonstration by their instructor, Mr Liddell, who stands with one foot raised against the blackboard in the centre of the photograph.

Opening of Byron Street Fire Station, 1940s. Shirebrook's first fire station was situated on Main Street early in the century, and remained in use until a new station building was erected by men of the National Fire Service on Byron Street during the 1940s. This building served Shirebrook for forty years, eventually being replaced by a modern station on Portland Road in 1986. Among the firemen and officials pictured here are Alan 'Micky' Duff (top left), the regular engine driver, Charles Coupe (in front of him), Mr G. Bamford, Fire Chief (centre) and Councillor Pickthorne (second right).

Langwith Junction ambulance class, 1908. Taking part in this early photograph session are: back row, left to right: T. North; F. Taylor; W. Bagshaw; H. Skinner; A. Bird; A. Youd. Middle row: B. Kidger; G. Wood; W. Wilkinson; T. Gittins; J. Thorpe; J. Horton; A. Jameson; R. Pegg. Front row: Dr P. Nettell (lecturer); T. Liddell (instructor and secretary); Master Roger Liddell (mascot); The man on the stretcher is S. Wood.

THE·BRITISH·RED·CROSS·SOCIETY

PRESIDENT
HER MAJESTY THE QUEEN

THIS IS TO CERTIFY THAT

R. Liddell

having attended a course of lectures and demonstrations in NURSING has been examined, and satisfied the Examiner in the said subject, in accordance with the regulations of the Society.

Examination Date 16·12·52

Where Held Mansfield

No.
C 30238

SECRETARY GENERAL

Red Cross Certificate in Nursing, awarded to Roger Liddell in 1952.

Ref. A.R.P./C. 3.

The Grand Priory in the British Realm
of the
Venerable Order of the Hospital of St. John of Jerusalem.
Ambulance Department.

The St. John Ambulance Brigade.

Air Raid Precautions and First Aid
for Air Raid Casualties.

This is to Certify

SUPERINTENDENT   THOMAS LIDDELL

Shirebrook Ambulance Division.

has been appointed a Brigade A.R.P. Instructor, Grade 2, vide Special Brigade Order of 31st October, 1935.

Date 9th April 1936.

Commissioner.

A.R.P. Certificate. Awarded to Superintendent Thomas Liddell, father of Roger, qualifying him as a Brigade A.R.P. Instructor (Grade 2) in 1936.

Langwith Junction Great Central Ambulance Class, 1910. Langwith Junction Station, originally part of the L.D. and E.C. line, was later taken over by the Great Central Railway. The 1910 Ambulance Class were winners of gold medals, the Maclure Bowl and Bartholomew Bowl. Back row, left to right: J. Thorpe; T. North; H. Hopkins. Front row, seated: Mr T. Liddell (Captain and lecturer) and T. Brett (right). Mr Liddell received an address of special thanks, signed by King George V.

A vital task. Miss Helen Bower testing a military motor-cycle, probably at the Standard Works at Coventry, during the First World War. Miss Bower, whose parents were licensees of the Victoria Hotel in the Model Village, is believed to have been the first woman appointed to inspect and test military motor vehicles at this time. She was married to H.W. Ruggins in 1917.

Colliery Ambulance Class, c. 1950. This picture, taken in the old Shirebrook Colliery canteen, celebrated the success of candidates in passing the Ambulance Examinations. Back row, left to right: Wilf Knowles; -?-; Jack Winstanley; Harry Shaw; Harry Roberts; -?-; Alf Young; Archie Machin; -?-; Arthur Cooper. Middle row: Johnny Price; -?-; -?-; Jack Turton; -?-; Fred Jackson; Mick Machin; Fred Sanders; George Taylor; unknown lady. Front row: Dixon Taylor (instructor); -?-; Bill Leadbeater; Bill Cox; 'Nock' Price; Mavis Burden; George Condon; ? Condon; -?-; ? Condon.

Serving with the Forces, 1. Nellie French (back row, third from left) with Army and A.T.S. colleagues at an unidentified military camp during the last war. Nellie, the first of her family to be born in Shirebrook, was posted to the South of England, and worked in stores and later in administration, attaining the rank of sergeant. She still lives in Shirebrook.

Serving with the Forces, 2. The late William Shaw (far right) in a moment of relaxation from his normal duties, while serving in Ceylon (now Sri Lanka) with the R.A.F. in 1943.

Shirebrook's Sunbeams, 1935. Members of the Shirebrook Salvation Army Sunbeams, a children's organization, on parade in the mid 1930s. Adjutant and Mrs Mitchell are on the left, and Sunbeam leaders Mr and Mrs F. Wall on the far right. The Sunbeams are; back row, left to right: Edna Riley; Mary Bailey; Gwen ?; Kitty Bailey; Lily Evans; Edith Riley; Irene Bills. Middle row: Peggy Gilbert; Rose Merry; Enid Wall; Joyce Smith; Marjorie Blount. Front row: Marjorie Allfree, Gwyneth Edmunds, Dorothy Smith, Joan Leadbeater.

Shirebrook Youth Club, 1950s. Members photographed at a party at St Joseph's Church. They include; back row, left to right: Bert Frear; Phil Barraclough; Cyril Birkin. Middle row: Roy Chapman; Alan Quemby (with curly hair); John Key; Harry Key; -?-; Malcolm Shaw. Jessie Dean is in the foreground on the right.

Salvation Army Scout Troop, 1930s. Scouts and Salvation Army officers outside the S.A. hut on Byron Street, in a pre-war group photograph.

Parish Church Scout Troop, 1930s. An unidentified group of scouts and officials assembled outside Holy Trinity Church. The clergyman (second row, fourth left) is the Rev. A.H. Hurt (father of the famous actor John Hurt), who was vicar of Shirebrook during the late 1930s. John Hurt spent his early childhood in the village.

On active service. Edwin Thomas ('Teddy') Bright, presents a neatly uniformed appearance to the studio photographer. Mr Bright saw action at Gallipoli in the First World War before returning to run the family business first established in the 1900s, which is still operating under new management at 5 King Edward Street.

Military duties. Henry Walter Ruggins in R.A.S.C. uniform during the First World War. Mr Ruggins, a native of Buckinghamshire, lived for over 50 years in Shirebrook, where at various times he was booking manager for the Empire, Superintendent of the Shirebrook Market, and a partner in the construction firm of F.H. & J.W. Moore. He died in 1952.

Mrs Harriet Benger. A well-known Shirebrook Salvation Army worker, pictured on the 'backs' of Victoria Street, off the Market Place. Beyond the row of buildings behind her is part of the embankment built by the Great Northern Railway for its Leen Valley Extension in the 1900s. In recent years the houses on Victoria Street have been replaced by shops, and the embankment has been removed.

An 'Angel' of 1940. Miss Joan Ruggins at the Mansfield Victoria Hospital, in 1940. The daughter of Mr H.W. Ruggins, Miss Ruggins (now Mrs G. Watts) was one of many nursing staff who provided medical care for wounded servicemen returning from Dunkirk. The sandbagged shelter in the background is a reminder of the ever-present threat of air raids.

Inspection, Church Drive. Sergeant William Eaton inspects the ranks of nursing and ambulance staff as they stand to attention opposite the entrance of Holy Trinity Church on Church Drive. The building to the left of the nurses is part of the old Council Depot, recently demolished, while at the foot of the slope Byron Street may be seen, with the fire station house to its left. In the distance behind the buildings it is possible to make out the Great Northern Railway embankment, which suggests a date some time in the 1970s.

Ambulancemen on parade, Skegness. This picture, too, is thought to date from the 1970s. Sergeant William Eaton is seen marching immediately behind the saluting officer, while in the main group further back are Arthur Cooper (far left) and Bill Philips (to the right of the corporal leading the group). The parade is following a route along Winthorpe Avenue towards the Derbyshire Miners' Holiday Camp.

Four

Holidays and Play

Seaside Stay. A group of Shirebrook holidaymakers outside their Blackpool hotel in 1948 or '49. The trip organiser, Phyllis Scott, is seated third from left, while in the back row are Henry Ashton (fourth right, in window) and Ambrose Stockdale (second right). Jimmy Scott is third right in the middle row, with Mrs Doris Stockdale second right.

Tea party, Congregational Hall. The Congregational Church on the crest of Church Drive was opened in 1905, and was the largest place of worship in the Model Village. This picture from the 1950s shows (front table, left side): Mrs Corden; Mr Harold Corden; Kenneth Roberts; Stan Bettison; Marjorie Ragsdale, June Allen, Winnie Lowe, -?-. Front table, right side: Mrs Caunt; Joe Hays; Mrs Hays; Mrs Lawrence; Bill Lawrence; Leslie Wilkinson; Mrs Wilkinson; Mrs Roper; Arthur Roper; Mrs Leverton; -?-. Top table, near side: -?-; Audrey Simpson; Dorothy Perkins; -?-; -?-. Far side: Barbara Corden; Joan Annibal; Janet Smith; -?-; -?-; Rev. Wilfred Walker (Congregational Minister).

Old Folks' Party, Gate Hotel. A group of local residents in party mood at Shirebrook's oldest working hostelry, some time during the 1970s. They are (left to right):Bill Gunston; Bob Sweet; Mrs Agnes Sweet; Ernest Roberts; Mrs Joyce Butler; Mrs Doan; Mrs Edith Butler; Johnny Spowage.

On Portland Road. A group of children confront the camera on the open ground lying off Portland Road, probably around 1950. The Station Hotel, which stands on the corner of Portland Road and Station Road, may be glimpsed in the background on the left.

On the backs. Children at large on the 'backs' behind the houses of Market Place and Ashbourne Street, near the village centre, around 1945. The latter street was one of several demolished in the 1970s. Shown here (left to right) are: Brian Peters; Wendy Holland; Lily Weaver; Shirley Holland; Jack Scruby; Irene Illsley; Kevin Holland; Richard Weaver; Maureen Scott; Derry Smith; Sandra Brown; Malcolm Scott.

The joys of camping, 1. Members of the Smith and Shaw families with Shirebrook Scouts at Skegness in the 1930s, wash up after an enjoyable meal.

The joys of camping, 2. And after the washing up, pose for the group photograph.

'Ladies' at the party, Austin Street. A group of (mainly) female revellers in the mood for a celebration. The disguised male exception is Mr Sid King, showing a fine pair of legs in the foreground. Also pictured are (left to right): Daisy Roden; Mary Brittles; Audrey Allsebrook; -?-; Mrs Fleming; Doris Roden; Mrs King; Audrey Spowage; Sylvia King; Amy Fleming; Lily Roden; June King; -?-; Ethel King.

Sportsmen at Boughton, 1928. A group of beaters pause for a photograph while helping with a shoot at Boughton in Nottinghamshire in 1928. Among the enthusiasts are Edward Cox (fourth from left); and Mr Reddish (fifth left).

Pals at the 'Soldiers', 1950s. Pals' outing from the Shirebrook ex-Servicemen's Club, some time after 1955. F. Cooney is behind the rest, on the steps of the coach. Back row, left to right: Dick Annibal; Bill Freeman; Alan Plevey; Joe Hardy; Tommy Parker; Bob Annibal; Bob Hibberd; Ken Dunstan; Walt Shaw; George Hall; Henry Stocks; E. Downes; V. Flemming; I. Pointon; H. Green; W. Moore; J. Wharton; B. Cotton; G. Plevey; P. Randall; A. Brickles. Front row: B. Ashall; W. Hall; A. Marchant; K. Hayden; R. Spencer; P. Hanrahan; E. Goddard; J. Siven; H. Scraton; J. Brittain.

Girls and dolls. Four young ladies guarding their dolls' pram outside the old flats at 41 Church Drive, Model Village, in the 1950s. Standing are Valerie Felse (left) and Anne Goddard (right); seated in front are Janet Hicken (left) and Lynda Roberts (right). The Model Village Infants' School is behind and to the left.

'Dead end kids'. Photographed on Portland Road during the 1950s. Back row, left to right: Peter Payne, Derek Shipley, ? Smith, ?, Roy Stubbs, Eunice Shipley, Margaret Shipley, Vera Shipley (née Valentine), Valerie Shipley. Front row: Michael Shipley, Lynda Roberts, Pat Shipley.

Bus ride. A man and a young boy board one of the familiar coaches run by the Shirebrook firm of William Truman and Son as it prepares to leave the village Market Place.

On tour. A Truman's coach makes a scheduled halt during a tour of Scotland some time in the '50s. Truman's provided Shirebrook with its main local bus service for many years, as well as organising holiday tours, before the firm finally sold out to East Midland Motor Services in 1956.

Ladies' outing. Three Shirebrook ladies explore the Skegness seafront in 1946. Left to right are: Mrs Woodhead, Mrs Anne Shaw, Mrs Doris Stockdale.

A family venture. Members of the Smith family of Shirebrook en route to the Skegness beaches in the 1950s.

All-male cast, 1. Taking it easy on the Isle of Man, '50s. Left to right: Bert White, Ben Cantrell, George Terry, George Jackson, Stan Glaydon.

All-Male Cast, 2. And further afield, in Barcelona. Left to right: Alan Green, Phil Clayton, Ben Cantrell, Malcolm Shaw.

Holiday group, Blackpool. Shirebrook holidaymakers on arrival at their Blackpool hotel, 1950s. Mrs Wileman, the trip organiser, is seated in the front row, third from left, Edna Dean on the far right. Doris Stockdale is on the far left in the second row, while on the back row are Phyllis Scott (second left) and Fred Cooke (fourth left).

Sookholme Dock. A pleasant rural area to the south-east of Shirebrook itself, Sookholme vied with Pleasley Vale as the favourite location for walks, picnics and courting assignations. Its low-lying nature rendered it subject to flooding, and it was popularly nicknamed 'Sookholme Dock'. This pre-war snapshot shows children at play in a temporary lake that has covered the road leading back to Shirebrook.

Beside the sea. Cyril Draycott (left) and Sam Allsop (right) relaxing on the dunes while on holiday at the seaside in the 1950s.

Skegness promenade. Malcolm Shaw (left) and Tommy Lievesley (right) on a tour of the front, with lollipops at the ready.

Pleasley Vale, 1950s. A local beauty spot within easy reach of the village, Pleasley Vale was a favoured location for walks and picnics. This 1950s shot shows Mrs Emma Roberts with her children (in ascending order) Peter, Lynda, and Harry.

Mother and son. Mrs Hilda Roberts and her son Harry at the Miners' Chalets, Skegness, in 1938. The wooden huts behind them were later to be used as billets for soldiers at the outbreak of the Second World War.

Sports Day, Skegness. A tight finish to the egg and spoon race. The photograph was taken in 1948 or 1949, when the Miners' Holiday Camp re-opened for the first time after the Second World War. Among the winners breasting the tape are Mary Middleton (now Mrs Oscroft, left) and Elsie Cartwright (right).

A closer look, 1950s. Master Peter Roberts sets out to explore his surroundings from the steps of his home on Linden Street.

Young men in their singlets, 1930s. A group of Shirebrook youngsters pictured at Skegness some time before the Second World War. Back row, left to right: Harold Jones, -?-, Bill Shaw. Front row: -?-, Cliff Jones, ? Jones.

Steam Traction Engine, Long Lane. This engine was the haulage unit for a threshing machine which was hired out in summer to the local farms. It is seen here making its way down Long Lane towards Carl Nicholson's garage, from which access was gained to the nearest of the fields. The low stone wall on the left, and the tell-tale structure of Shirebrook Police Station on the right, help to confirm the location. The visit of the threshing machine was an exciting event for Shirebrook youngsters, who followed its progress while playing in the fields during the '30s and '40s.

Girls and motorcycle, Morris Street. Marjorie Stanley is at the controls in this unusual 'action shot', with her friend Evelyn Douds riding pillion. The young girl on the far left of the picture, taken in 1946 or 1947, is Rita Morphus. Morris Street, which adjoined Station Road near the Market Place, was one of five demolished in the early 1970s.

Five

Schools and Scholars

Staff and pupils of Carter Lane Girls' School, 1928.

Whaley Thorns School Football Team, 1952–53. Situated in the neighbouring village of Langwith, Whaley Thorns is an area with its own distinct identity. This early 1950s team consists of; back row, left to right: Mr Sharpe, A. Carrington, L. Mitchell, G. Smith, N. Wright, S. Latchen, I. Thomas, Mr Frost. Front row: J. Bennett, D. Roberts, ? Widdowson, A. Errington, C. Brookes, ? Cartwright, ? Wilson.

Model Village Infants, 1910. One of the earliest shots of Model Village Infants. The Model Village schools were established between 1907 and 1910, to accommodate the growing number of school age children as Shirebrook's population continued to increase. As yet, this group of pupils and their teachers remains unidentified.

Class 3A, Carter Lane, 1945-46. Miss Bacon (teacher) is on the far left, and Mr Atkin (headmaster) on the right. Pupils are; back row, left to right: B. Clay, R. Woodhead, K. Smith, J. Thomas, W. Betts, D. Peel, R. Burnbanks, B. Simms, A. Burden, G. Sindall, J. Miller, L. Brittain. Middle row: M. Judd, D. Parker, T. Wilson, K. Morgan, R. Yates, J. Randall, R. Drabble, J. Mantle, R. Gorrill, A. Patterson, J. Paling, E. Lound, ? Lunn, D. Potts. Front row: R. Condon, A. Wheatley, G. Bradbury, S. Lucas, L. Parker, J. Bown, M. Platts, ? Purdon, B. Gibbons, F. Freeman, B. Frith.

Carter Lane 'A' Football Team, 1946/7. Mr Atkin (headmaster) stands at the rear on the left, and Mr Bailey (teacher) on the right. The team are; back row, left to right: W. Betts, G. Ashall, R. York, C. Goodwin, A. Hillsley, G. Bradbury. Front row: R. Condon, R. Woodhead, K. Morgan, ? Donaldson, K. Hardwick, F. Turton.

East Derbyshire School Sports, 4 July 1950. Model Village school team with trophy. Back row, left to right: Mr E. Wright (teacher), J. Garbett, J. Bayliss, Mr C. Reay (headmaster), T. Brown, C. Goodwin, Mr Birkumsher (teacher). Middle row: D. Shepherd, R. Stubbs, A. Lound, G. Pearce, M. Peters, K. Smith, L. Barnes. Front row: G. Bradbury, O. Nurse, B. Frith, R. Cann, G. Bright, A. Birch.

Model Village Schools Eleven, 1948/9. Mr Birkumsher (left) and Mr Wright (right). Back row, left to right: Higginson, Foster, Hatton, Wake, Lound, Hunt, Jowse. Front row: Godfrey, Spencer, Walker, Lound, Bradbury, Dean, Holland, Jackson.

Girls' hockey team, 1937. Members of the hockey team at Shirebrook County Secondary School for Girls, more popularly known as Miss Wills' School in 1937. Back row, left to right: Gwen Joynes (Shirebrook), Doris Fretwell (Shirebrook), Mary Wholley (Palterton), Renee Kirk (Creswell), Nancy Clarke (Shirebrook), Sylvia Farraday (Clowne). Front row: Doreen Robinson (Shirebrook), Kathleen Ward (Shirebrook) Jessie Peake (Shirebrook), Jessie Peake (Shirebrook), Dorothy Formston (Langwith Junction), Frances Williams (Elmton).

Carter Lane Sports Team, 1930s. Founded as the Board Schools in the 1890s, Carter Lane Schools were built in response to the arrival of the many families who flocked to Shirebrook following the sinking of the colliery. Like most schools of the period, there was a strong emphasis on sport, and this unidentified sports team is one example of many.

Carter Lane Junior Boys, 1939. Sporting team with trophy. Back row, left to right: Ward, Mr Atkin (headmaster), G. York, Mr Wheatley (teacher), H.Wragg. Front row: A. Cooper, P. Charlesworth, F. Hall, R. Kyte, S. Smith.

Edward Cox at Carter Lane, c. 1900. A much earlier shot of a class at the Carter Lane Board Schools at the turn of the century. The late Edward Cox (1893-1974) is shown third from right in the second row. According to his testimony, the boy holding his cap (third row, second left) could be smelt a mile away, which may explain the concerned expressions of some of his fellow pupils!

East Derbyshire Boys v. Boston. A team photograph, probably dating from the early 1920s, and showing; left to right: A. Crowe (Model Village), ? Thorpe (Warsop Vale), A. Cutts (Model Village) E. Smith (Model Village), T. Ashmore (Carter Lane), ? Nicholas (Warsop Vale), L. Smith (Langwith), ? Binney (Carter Lane), George Bowater (Carter Lane), C. Elliott (Scarcliffe). George Bowater later played for Shirebrook F.C. in their last three seasons in the Midland League, and both he and Ernest Smith saw service in the Football League.

Six

The People

Family snapshot. Cecil James French, with his wife, Lil, and their son Michael, at Bovington Army Camp in 1942. Mr French, who still lives in Shirebrook, was an Army tank instructor and Area lightweight boxing champion, and met his wife – who escaped from occupied Jersey – while stationed in the south.

Brother and sister. George Hall (above)
and (below) his sister Rose Hall, probably
photographed about 1940. The Halls
once lived at the Rock Cottages, some of
Shirebrook's oldest residences, which have
since been demolished.

Mr and Mrs Yates, Rock Cottages. The couple are believed to be the last people to have occupied the Rock Cottages prior to their demolition.

Entrepreneurs, Central Drive. An early picture, showing Mr F. Coupe (left) and Joseph Cox (right) outside the premises of Mr Coupe's undertaking business at the bottom of Central Drive, adjoining the smithy of Levi Elvidge. Mr Cox owned a team of horses which he hired to Mr Coupe for funeral processions.

A child at school. A youthful Edward Cox (first left, third row) at the age of five, in the Infant Class at Carter Lane School, in 1898. Mr Cox, who died in 1974, worked for many years as a roadsweeper for the local council.

A child at play. A picture from the 1900s, showing Edward Cox standing to the left, with his hand on the rump of the donkey. The scene was shot behind the bullock shed at Church Farm, Main Street, which was later demolished.

Mr Martin and family. Mr Frank Martin (on far left) served as an Army sergeant in the First World War, and as a special constable in the Second World War. He was better known to most as caretaker of the Shirebrook Colliery Offices. Mr Martin's daughter, Doris Martin, is on the far right of the picture.

Ladies and child, Prospect Drive. Edna Palmer, Ivy Palmer, a young Ernest Roberts and his mother Mrs Hilda Roberts, in a group portrait. The photograph is believed to have been taken at Prospect Drive in the Model Village, around 1928.

Wedding group, Warren Terrace. Warren Terrace is the name given to the row of houses at the western end of Main Street, where the village adjoins the Pleasley Road. The wedding group photograph was taken at the rear of No. 12 Warren Terrace, shortly after the marriage of Wilfred Allen and Minnie Otter. Back row, left to right: Doris Allen, Harold Mellor, Mrs Allen, -?-, Mrs Otter, -?-, Alfred Allen, Walter Lee. Seated, front, are the groom, Wilfred Allen, and the bride, Minnie Otter. The young bridesmaid in the front row is Violet Flint.

A butcher at work, Sookholme. The Shirebrook butcher Walter Flint (right) with a colleague and two healthy-looking beasts no doubt destined for slaughter, on the corner of Longster Lane, Sookholme, near Sookholme Farm, on the south-eastern outskirts of the village.

Flint family wedding. One of the oldest established Shirebrook families, Flint's butchers' business dates back to the 1890s, and has only recently passed out of the family's hands. This early photograph was taken in the yard behind what is now Ashley's butcher's shop on Main Street, and celebrates the wedding of Nellie Flint to Harry Fox of Clowne. William Flint, sixth left on the back row, was a butcher on Main Street, while Alice Mills (née Flint, second left, third row) ran a sweet shop at the corner of Patchwork Row and King Edward Street, and Gertrude Paling (née Flint, third left) kept a pork butcher's shop on Main Street. The gentleman in the smock standing second right, is William Flint, reputedly the first butcher in Shirebrook. His second wife, Ann Flint, is seated fourth left in the second row, to the right of the bride and groom.

A well-dressed landlord. Mr Frank Baines, landlord of the Market Hotel in 1908, strikes an impressive pose in his Sunday best while en route to some official function.

Children and pets, 1950s. Members of the Shipley family with their pet dogs on Portland Road. Margaret Shipley is on the far right, with Brenda Shipley to her left. The small boy at the front is Derek Shipley, and behind him is his brother Clarence.

Husband and wife. Harry Gilbert and his wife, Maria (second row, third and fourth from left) at the centre of a family group dating from around 1920. Mr Gilbert, who ran a shoemaking business in the village, was also a well-known figure in the Salvation Army church and scout group.

Warren Terrace Ride. Mr Spencer (on right) keeps a hold on the horse, while his two sons, John (centre) and Bob (left) enjoy the ride, on open ground at the back of the family home at 56 Warren Terrace. John later worked for the local council, while Bob was a miner at Warsop Main Colliery, and was also known as a useful cricketer.

A time to remember. Thomas Nicholson Wright (on the left) and his sister Winifred (right) with their mother, some time in the 1890s. Thomas was then 2 ½ years old, and his sister one year old. Sadly, Thomas was killed in action near Ypres on 19 October 1917.

Mr and Mrs Frederick French. A studio portrait from the 1950s. Mr French was one of many workers who came to Shirebrook from the West Midlands in the 1900s in search of employment.

Mr French and Sons, 1930s. A family snapshot showing Mr Frederick French, Sr. (centre) with sons Frederick Jr. (left) and Cecil James (right) on allotments not far from the centre of the village. The colliery aerials may be seen in the background.

Joffre Kitchener French. In his Army uniform, in the early 1940s. Mr French, also a son of Frederick French Sr., worked for many years in Shirebrook Colliery Offices. He died in 1978.

Left: Brother and sister, Victoria Hotel. Miss Helen Bower (far left) and her brother Ernest Bower (second left) with staff of the Victoria Hotel, some time between 1910 and 1914. Built in 1897 by the Shirebrook Colliery Co., the 'Vic' was the only public house in the Model Village, and their father, Ernest C. Bower, was its licensee.

Left: At ease in France. Jack Wootton (front, left) and his friend Frank Oakton (right) with fellow-soldiers in camp in France during the First World War. Sadly, Jack Wootton was later killed by an exploding shell.

French family gathering, 1950. Taken to celebrate the Silver Wedding Anniversary of Mr and Mrs Ernest French, on 26 December 1950. Back row, (left to right): Mr Joffre K. French, Mrs Lil French, Mrs Edna French (now Mrs P. Banks), Mrs Ada French, Mr Frederick French, Jr., Mrs Florence Buckley (née French), Mr Harry Buckley, Mrs Lucy Revill (née French), Mr Walter Revill, Mrs Nellie Watkinson (née French), Mr Fred Watkinson. Middle row: Mr Frederick French, Sr., Mrs Minnie French, Mr Ernest French, Mrs Lil French. Front row: Pamela French (now Mrs R. Crutchley) Carol French (now Mrs P. Stansfield), Michael French, Christopher Watkinson, Jennifer Watkinson (now Mrs G. Sadler), Anne Buckley (now Mrs P. Utridge).

Carl Nicholson. The descendant of a local landowning family, whose brother Claude also farmed in Shirebrook, Carl Nicholson is better known as the founder and proprietor of the Central Garage, which he established on Central Drive in 1924. A keen sportsman in his younger days, he was a regular forward with Shirebrook Wednesday F.C., and also played several games for Shirebrook Football Club in the Central Alliance during the early 1920s. Here he is seen testing out a motor-cycle on his garage forecourt. The man standing on the right of the picture is Mr Archibald Brewster.

Mr Pickbourne. A mechanic at Carl Nicholson's garage, Mr Pickbourne (on the right) is here photographed with an unknown colleague, probably in 1925.

A Model Village Gathering. The event (if any) has not been identified, but the ladies in the picture are, left to right: Betsy Collier, Sheila Burns, Mary Kelly, May Hawson, Rita Hawson, Olive Collier, Irene Bull, and Joyce Burns.

Alan 'Micky' Duff. 'Micky' served with Carl Nicholson in the Army during the First World War, and returned to Shirebrook to work as foreman in the Central Garage in the 1920s. He also drove passengers on paid excursions to Matlock and similar tourist spots on Carl's behalf, and was driver of the engine for the Shirebrook Fire Brigade. In addition to these impressive talents, he was an effective saxophonist.

Melville and Wilma Warriner, c. 1920. Melville's father, Samuel Warriner, was a musical instrument dealer and a talented engineer, with premises off the Market Place; reputedly the first man to own a car in Shirebrook, he set up an omnibus service which failed following the 1926 Strike. Melville, seen here with his sister Wilma, worked as a bus driver with Truman's and East Midland Motor Services before gaining a higher position. He entered local government, where he enjoyed a distinguished career with Warsop U.D.C. and later with Mansfield District Council, where he was Chairman during the Queen's Jubilee visit of 1977. He died in November 1977, aged 63.

A grand day out. A group of 'regulars' muster outside the Great Northern Hotel, Main Street, prior to departure for the Manchester November Handicap Races, in the late 1940s or early '50s. Left to right are: Albert Daniels, Les Clay, Frank Buckley, Jimmy Wilson, Ron Holland, Mr Pears, Dick Dillon, Herbert Phillips, -?-, Joe Collier, Henry Pears, Walter Woolley, Harry Webster, Arthur Walker (landlord), Joe Lyons, Willie Preston, George Hall, Freddie Comery, George Naylor, George Scott, unknown, Freddie Smith (in cap), Joe Dillon, Freddie Bullars, Walter Brewin, Horace Yates, Bill Palmer. At the rear, by the bus, are Sam Allsop, Tom Holland and Dennis Comery, while aboard the vehicle is Kevin Holland.

Harry and Jane Thompson. A picture taken in the early 1900s. Harry Thompson, who is believed to be the first baker in Shirebrook, arrived in the village from his native Rutland at the turn of the century, and set up his business on Nicholson's Row. It later became part of the premises for Grainger's decorating and ironmongery business.

Lily Flint. A studio portrait from early in the century. Lily, a member of the well-known butchers' family, was to become Mrs Alfred Williams.

Right: Miss Susan Allen. A photograph taken some time before her marriage to the Shirebrook butcher Walter Flint.

Below: Jon Schofield. Although born in Beeston, Nottinghamshire, John Schofield has strong ties with Shirebrook, which was the birthplace of his mother, Edna Schofield, and most of her sisters. Jon's television career began with set designing for Emergency, Ward 10, and he went on to produce shows for Tom Jones and Engleber Humperdinck for the U.S. market, and also devised and directed the popular comedy show *Who Do You Do?*. Here he is pictured with several of his Shirebrook relatives. Back row, left to right: Mr Robert Blake (uncle), Mrs Schofield (wife), Tracey Schofield (daughter). Front row: Mrs Lil Huntingdon, Mrs Eva Davies, Mrs Vera Waterman, Mrs Annie Saunderson, Mrs Elsie Blake. The five ladies at the front are all aunts of Mr Schofield, daughters of Mr and Mrs Evans of Austin Street, and all but Mrs Saunderson were born in Shirebrook.

George Evans. Pictured in front of his house on Church Drive, Model Village, in the 1950s. Mr Evans later served with the Chesterfield Police Force, and afterwards as a driver with East Midland Motor Services.

Best behaviour, 1930s. Four Shirebrook schoolboys in an unusually well-dressed and formal pose. The youngster at the front is Joseph Collier, with Sammy Cantrell standing to his left and Gordon Eames on his right. The boy behind Joe Collier is Colin Eames.

Dr David Sutherland. The son of an Edinburgh headmaster and himself a distinguished academic scholar, Dr Sutherland came to Shirebrook in 1909, having previously worked as a surgeon at Worksop Hospital. During his fifteen years in Shirebrook, he built up a highly successful practice and involved himself in the life of the community, becoming a loved and respected figure in Shirebrook society. A keen sportsman, he was for several years chairman of Shirebrook Football Club, and gave medical assistance when their goalkeeper Joseph Orme fractured his leg in a match on the Langwith Road ground. Dr Sutherland volunteered for military service in 1915, and saw action as a naval surgeon aboard HMS *Implacable* in the Eastern theatre of the war. After three years of war he was invalided home, suffering from malaria, which eventually contributed to his death at the age of 46 in February 1924. Following one of the largest funerals held in Shirebrook, where the cortège is said to have extended for a quarter of a mile, he was buried in Shirebrook cemetery. Dr Sutherland, pictured here in his naval uniform during the First World War, is still remembered with great affection by Shirebrook people.

Granny Hicken. A well-known Shirebrook character, Granny Hicken was born Decima Hurst in Leicestershire in the 1860s. Following her marriage to the coal miner Thomas Hicken, she moved to Hucknall Torkard in Nottinghamshire, and from there to Shirebrook, where the family settled in the Model Village built by the Shirebrook Colliery Co. A hard-working, charismatic figure, she took in washing from Mr Coupe the undertaker to help keep the family she raised, and remained a respected local character until her death. Granny Hicken is pictured here in her later years, at her home at 80 Vale Drive, Model Village, during the 1930s.

In repose. Helen Bower (seated) with unknown friend, a pleasing studio portrait taken in the year 1911.

Philip Bilzon. Born and raised in Shirebrook, Phillip won awards for solo dramatic presentations at the Mansfield and Nottingham Arts Festivals, and also earned recognition as a talented local actor and director in performances of *Billy Liar* and *Educating Rita* at the Mansfield Community Theatre. He obtained an Honours Degree in Creative Arts at Newcastle Polytechnic and a Diploma in Drama Therapy at St Albans, and is currently lecturing at Watford College of Further Education while studying for a teaching diploma. For several years a member of Shirebrook & District Writers' Group, he is shown taking part in a performance reading at Northern College, Barnsley, in October 1989.

Colin Tarrant. A native of Shirebrook, where his father, Mr H. Tarrant, kept the VG store on the corner of Victoria Street, off the Market Place, Colin studied drama and gained experience in street theatre before going on to win wider fame as a television actor. He played a leading role in the TV adaptation of D.H. Lawrence's novel *The Rainbow*, some of the scenes being filmed in nearby Carr Vale, and is even better known to viewers as Inspector Andrew Monroe in the popular ITV police series *The Bill*. He continues a tradition of notable actors born in Shirebrook begun earlier by John Hurt, son of the local vicar Rev. A.H. Hurt in the 1930s.

Seven

The Sporting Life

Shirebrook Colliery Cricket Club Dinner, 1930s. Back row, left to right: Robert Hays, -?-, Joseph Hays, Bob Collins, -?-, -?-, H. Baker. Front row: Alfred Naylor, Mr Naylor, Joe Charlton, captain (second right, holding trophy), Henry Murt (far right).

Shirebrook Athletic F.C., 1927/8. A lesser team, not to be confused with the better-known Shirebrook Football and Athletic Club, who represented the village in the Central Alliance and Midland League, this unidentified group is typical of the minor sides active in Shirebrook before the Second World War.

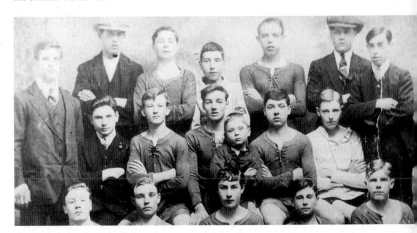

Shirebrook Norwood Rangers, 1920/21. A side which took its name from Norwood Crossings in nearby Langwith, where their pitch was situated. Back row, left to right: S. Fannen (Secretary), E. Walsh, W. Betteridge, W. Bennett, B. Bennett, J. Charlesworth, D. Kerry. Middle row: J. Harris, B. Hall, J. Camm, S. Bennett, G. Mitchell, G. Fannan, Jr. (mascot). Front row: J. Eaton, J. Milburn, T. Lee, B. Whitworth, A. Bennington.

Shirebrook Youth Club Football Team, 1949/50. Back row, left to right: J. Sills, K. Wake, A. Frith, M. Higginson, R. Plant, K. York. Front row: F. Heaver, M. Shaw, L. Creswell, W. Dodds, H. Swift.

Shirebrook Youth Club Football Team, 1952. Photographed outside Langwith Bassett School. Back row, left to right: J. Holland, P. Whatmore, K. Wake, D. Middleton, M. Higginson, B. Dean, B. Bills. Front row: J. Shore, C. Gay, C. Cann, A. Land, T. Hunt.

Holy Trinity Church Cricket Club, 1911. A magnificent portrait of the Shirebrook parish church cricket team, a side less well known today but containing several familiar names. Back row, left to right: H. Close, G.W. Wagstaffe, Albert Turton. Middle row: J. Sansom (umpire), G. Whitelaw, A. Evans, G.H. Redsell, F. Turton (scorer). Front row: T. Ward, Alfred Turton (vice-captain), H.W. Ruggins (captain) E.W. Ogden (Hon. Sec.), J. Fowler. G. Whitelaw was associated with the Shirebrook Colliery Cricket Club, while Mr Ogden was a committee man with Shirebrook White Star F.C. The Turton family are closely linked with the history of the parish church, with Mrs Mabel Turton receiving the M.B.E. for her years of service as church organist, while captain H.W. Ruggins was to become better known as a partner in F.H. & J.W. Moore, Market Superintendent, and booking manager at the Empire theatre.

Langwith Junction Wagon Works of W.H. Davis & Sons was established on Langwith Road in the 1890s, close to the L.D. & E.C. Railway Station (later Great Central), and was a major employer in the village. The photograph shows one of the company's early teams with their trophies.

Langwith Junction Wagon Works F.C., 1930s. A more recent Wagon Works side, probably photographed in 1937. Back row, left to right: Jack Marrows, Walter Allen (goalkeeper), Sam Shepherd, Bert Randall, John Charles. Middle row: Fred Walker, Walter Davis. Front row: Clarence V. Cadman, Eric Adams, Fred Garner, 'Zeke' Bowater, Freddie Thorsen (captain).

Shirebrook White Star, 1913/14. A well-known local side whose pitch was located on the south-east side of the village, between Vernon Street and Sookholme. The two players fourth and fifth from left in the back row are believed to be Robinson and Easom, Wilf Ogden is the second committee man from the right.

Shirebrook Colliery Cricket Club, 1938 or 1939. Shirebrook Colliery Cricket Club was begun in 1899, and quickly established a strong local reputation, winning the Rayner Cup six times between 1923 and 1942 . The team is pictured here on the Colliery Recreation Ground. Back row, left to right: -?-, D. Griffiths, M. Cutts, H. Elliott, E. Hunt, B. Collins. Front row: Ron Hays, -?-, J. Platts, J. Charlton, captain (with trophy), A. Palmer, R. Gilbert, J. Simpson.

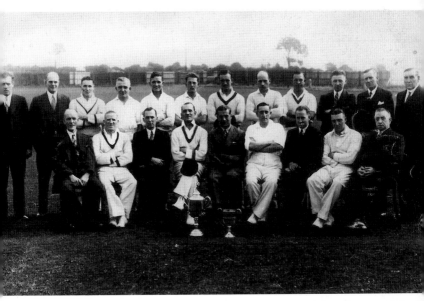

Shirebrook Colliery Cricket Club, 1942. The Derbyshire League and Rayner Cup winning side, once more photographed on the Colliery Recreation Ground. Back row, left to right: A. Parker, E. Hunt, F. Shaw, H. Baker, G. Elliott, R. Gilbert, R. Hays, J. Platts, J. Simpson, E. Wilkinson, ?, Bob Wilson (landlord, Victoria Hotel). Front row: B. Collins, A. Palmer, M. Hurt, J. Charlton (captain), A.E. Naylor (colliery agent manager), D. Griffiths, H. Knighton (colliery manager), J. Shooter, W. Wilkinson.

Shirebrook Byron Albion, 1909/10. An early team photograph showing one of Shirebrook's lesser-known sides on the Park Road Recreation Ground. Edward Cox is on the front row to the far left.

East Derbyshire boys, 1953-4. A group photograph taken at Carter Lane School. The teacher on the left is Mr Jones. A young Barry Lyons, seated in the centre of the front row with the ball appropriately placed at his feet, was later to become one of the most famous modern Shirebrook football players, with an illustrious career at Rotherham, Nottingham Forest, and York City. His talents, however, were very much part of a family footballing tradition.

Joe Lyons off duty. Joe Lyons, father of Philip and Barry Lyons, earned a notable reputation as a goalscoring centre-forward with Shirebrook Warren Terrace in the 1940s and '50s. Warren Terrace were one of the village's longest-established clubs, with their ground opposite the houses on the western edge of Shirebrook in use from the 1900s, and in Joe's time with them won many trophies in local competitions. Joe Lyons, who once scored 100 goals in a season, and 17 in a single game, was offered a trial with Arsenal on leaving school, but was obliged to decline for financial reasons. He is shown here in a moment of relaxation on open ground behind the family home. Warren Terrace itself may be seen in the background.

Warren Terrace, 1951. Joe Lyons and team members on the Warren Terrace football ground. The road behind and to the left is Common Lane. Back row, left to right: K. Cantrell, F. Woodlands, D. Clarke, D. Wheatley, A. Cantrell, G. Bonsall, G. Cooper, W. Knight. Front row: E. Hindson, J. Hall, 'Nobby' Pointon, Joe Lyons, Syd Taylor, T. Whitehead, and an unknown referee.

Byron Boys, Park Road, 1960s. Barry Lyons graduated from school football to play with Shirebrook Byron Boys F.C., who were based at the Park Road Recreation Ground. Barry is the player on the left of the three in the foreground, all of whom wear the club's green and white strip.

Barry Lyons in action. Barry was signed by 2nd Division Rotherham United in 1962, and remained with them until 1966. This exciting action shot was taken during this period. Barry moved to Nottingham Forest, where he excelled as a stylish wing player for seven seasons, his side finishing as runners up in the 1st Division in 1972. Following spells with York City and Darlington, and two years in football management, he retired from the game, and now runs a hotel in York.

A promising talent. Philip Lyons, Barry's brother, emerged from schoolboy football as a gifted and skilful player with a promising future in the game. In this early team photograph he is the youngster seated 3rd left in the front row, with his cousin Graham Charlesworth fourth left beside him. Philip Lyons starred with Alfreton Town, and was later signed by Lincoln City, but a serious leg injury sadly ended his football career. He has subsequently made a second, equally successful career in the catering business.

An Official Function. Barry Lyons, as guest of honour, receives the keys to the new Warren Terrace Changing Rooms from Councillor Harold Butt (on right) at the official re-opening ceremony in the 1970s. Councillor Mrs E. Bennett stands next to Mr Lyons, and Councillor Mrs Binney by Mr Butt, while in the background of the picture are Councillor Bentley, Councillor Mrs Storey, and Councillor J. Wilson (on right).

Shirebrook F.C., 1950s. Pictured on the Welfare (later B.R.S.A.) ground, Langwith Road. The Langwith Road School buildings may be seen in the background. Back row, left to right: H. Marriott (treasurer, 3rd left), unkown, S. Parker, T. Whitehead, A. Price, S. Flewitt, V. Hill. Front row: R. Coggan (assistant trainer), H. Walters, A. Williams, W. Atkins, G. Bushby, W. Roberts, H. Turton (trainer), P. Turton (mascot).

A foiled attack. Shirebrook goalkeeper Roy Hunt makes a timely save in a hard-fought game in the fourth qualifying round of the F.A. Cup between Shirebrook F.C. and Boston United, played in 1953 on the Langwith Road ground. In spite of his tireless efforts, Boston eventually went through as winners by 5 goals to 2.

F.A. Cup side, 1953. Members of the Shirebrook F.C. side who met Boston United in the 4th qualifying round of the F.A. Cup. Back row, left to right: W. Eaton (Secretary), H. Walters, G. Bushby, R. Smith, R. Hunt, S. Flewitt, G. Simmonds. Front row: D. Kimberley, ? Reist, K. Sansom, F. Hopkins, A. Land, H. Turton (trainer), ? Furniss (mascot).

A priceless shot. Kenny Sansom (right foreground) breaks through to drive in the vital goal against Central Alliance champions Ilkeston Town in the Derbyshire Divisional Cup Final, played on the Baseball Ground, Derby, on April 16th (Good Friday) 1954. The goal was enough to gain victory for Shirebrook, and secured them the Derbyshire Senior Cup.

Eight

Ceremonies and Celebrations

Fancy dress carnival, 1931. A youthful Miss Kathleen Scruby enters as 'The Pit Boy'. Fancy dress carnivals were a regular feature of village life in the 1930s.

Royal visit, 1914. One of a large number of photographs taken to commemorate the visit to Shirebrook of King George V and Queen Mary in the first year of the First World War. The photographer was S. Hill of 110 Station Road, and the picture shows one side of the Market Place, with the Post Office on the left, and in the centre the grocery store of A.B. Gibson, which was to close a few years later.

Wedding Day, Victoria Hotel. A large wedding party assembles for the group photograph in the yard of the hotel. Miss Helen Bower is the bridesmaid standing to the right of the (unknown) bride in the centre of the picture, which was taken some time before her own marriage in 1917.

Something of importance. A large crowd gathers in Shirebrook Market Place for an unspecified event, which may or may not be the aforementioned royal visit. Certainly the dress of the spectators appears to date from the same period. Shirebrook's Market square is undoubtedly large for a place of its size, and was the regular venue for the annual October fairs or 'feasts' before the Second World War.

Princesses and Bandsmen. A photograph taken around 1960, possibly at a carnival or beauty contest. The 'Princesses' are believed to be Miss State (left) and Miss Court (on the right), and Mrs Court is the lady standing second from right. The bandsmen (and friends) are: left to right; Les Lee, -?-, Herbert Bayliss, Graham Place, Joe Answer, Mr Court, -?-, Derek Neale, -?-, -?-, Mr Davis?, -?-.

Scholars rewarded. Presentation of diplomas at the Model Village School during the 1950s. Mr Reay (headmaster, on far left) presents the award to Robert Amos. Mrs Lunn is third from left, Mrs Latham seated second right, and Mrs Florence Spencer standing at far right, while other pupils include John Plant (4th right), Alfred Benger (2nd right), and ? Evans (standing behind John Plant).

Tom Faulkner's Dance Band, 1930s, pictured at an unidentified venue. Tom was brother of the more famous Charlie Faulkner, and was also known as a bandleader in the Shirebrook area before the war.

Opening of the Pentecostal Mission. The Mission on Manvers Street was built around 1950, and the opening ceremony attracted a large attendance. Local musician Archie Roberts plays for the occasion to the crowd, who are; back row left to right: Alan Warriner, Pastor Davis (Mansfield Pentecostal Church), Archie Roberts (playing accordian), Mrs Betts, Mrs Martin, Miss Jones, Pastor Foster. Third row: Rev. Horner (Chesterfield), Mrs Brittain, Mrs Gunton, Mrs Wisher, Ivy Wisher. Second row: Mrs Langley, Mrs Saunderson, John Saunderson, Mrs Hilda Roberts, Father Moggs (seated), Mrs Moggs, Mrs Edmunds, -?-, Harry Roberts. Front row: June Gunton, Doug Saunderson, Mrs A. Saunderson, Harry Saunderson, Mrs Roberts, -?-, Mrs Wilkinson, Joe Lunn.

A bandmaster dies. The funeral of Joseph Levick, Shirebrook's long-serving bandmaster, in 1954. Under Mr Levick's leadership, the Shirebrook Silver Band won prizes in local and national competitions over a period of years. Here Sgt Wilfred Bodsworth (in uniform on right) directs the *cortège* from the Bourne Methodist Church, Main Street, after the funeral service. Pallbearers in view are Joe Answer (front), Derek Neale (centre) and Alan Floyde (rear).

Band in procession. Shirebrook Band accompanies the funeral procession through the Market Place, where an assembled crowd stands to watch them pass. The Market Hotel or 'Drum' may be seen on the far right, while on the left are the shops of G.T. Slaney and E. Williamson. Further back, along Station Road, a single-deck and double-deck coach wait for the procession to move on.

Ezra Read Pianoforte Tutor. Ezra Read, who spent the last ten years of his life in Shirebrook, playing at the 'Empire' and 'Town Hall' theatres, was world-famous as the composer of piano tutors which enjoyed phenomenal sales. One such tutor even appeared in a silent film. Ezra Read is buried in Shirebrook.

Easter Presentation Concert, 1937. Poster advertising forthcoming concert at the 'Empire' on Station Road, headlined by Shirebrook Silver Prize Band and featuring other local entertainers.

First Class Certificate. Presented by the London College of Music to Miss Beatrice Nora Parker, pupil of Miss Mabel Shepherd, for passing the Primary Examination, on 22 December 1926.

Out on the town. Ernest and Emma Roberts dance the night away at Charlie Faulkner's 'Elite' Ballroom on Main Street (Patchwork Row) in the 1950s.

Long Service Awards, Langwith Junction. Mr Blundell, District Superintendent, presents gold watches to a group of railway workers at the Langwith Junction Depot in the 1940s. Left to right are: H. Watts, T. Dernley, G. Steele, J. Square, G. Matthews, unknown Tuxford driver, union steward, and A. Hill.

Carnival fun, 1934. Miss Kathleen Scruby (in white dress, on right), with her decorated ice cream float, in Shirebrook Market Place. Behind the interested onlookers is the Market Hotel with its advert for Shipstone's Ales.

Mrs Hill presents .... The late Mrs B.A. Hill (standing third from right, front row) presents a handbag to Mrs Gough, at an unidentified function believed to have taken place at the Social Service Centre, Nicholson's Row, possibly during the 1960s. Miss Hodson and Mrs Jackson are seated first and second left, and standing behind them are Mrs Hubbard and Councillor Mrs E. Bennett. Councillor Harold Butt is far left in the third row, with Mrs Pacey third left and Mrs Bettison, far right. Councillor B. Robinson is on the far right in front of the Woodbine advert, and third left in the back row is Councillor H. Hubbard.

Carnival Parade, Langwith Road. Watched by a large crowds of both adults and children, a drum major leads the white-uniformed band along Langwith Road towards the Recreation Ground. The buildings of Langwith Road School (opened as the Central School in 1929) may be seen on his right. The Langwith Road Recreation Ground (now the B.R.S.A.) is still a venue for band competitions, carnivals, fairs and sporting events today. Judging by the dress of the spectators, this picture was probably taken in the 1950s or early 1960s.

Youth Club Christmas Party, 1950s. Group photograph at St Joseph's Church, Langwith Road. Back row, left to right: -?-, Roy Plant, Malcolm Shaw, Jessie Dean, Derek Jackson, Peter Bennett. Front row: -?-, -?-, Jimmy Widdowson (wearing hat), Harry Key, L. Creswell, Michael Higginson, Bill Salmon (youth club leader, as Santa Claus) embracing Mr Court (far right).

Shirebrook Youth Club Band. Taken at a Christmas Party, 1949. Left to right are: A. Coggin (trumpet), E. Tuffrey (accordion), G. Lee (trombone), W. Dodds (piano), G. Wells (drums), H.Chambers (violin).

Carnival Queen and attendants, 1960s. Photographed at Langwith Road Recreation Ground. The school buildings may be seen in the background. Left to right are: Glenda Bayliss, Jean Gilbert (Carnival Queen, centre) and Cath Robinson (later Mrs Hibberd).

VE Day preparations. Trimmings are hung up at Ashbourne Street in readiness for the celebrations.

VE party, Ashbourne Street. Parents and children assemble for the group photograph, while more spectators gather in the doorways of the terraced houses on either side.

VE Day street party, Devonshire Street. A joyous crowd of Devonshire Street residents and friends prepare to celebrate Victory in Europe with a welcome meal at tables laid along the street. Guest of honour, at the head of the table in the foreground, is Joe Collier, still in uniform. Mr Collier had been a P.O.W. in Stalag VIIIB in Germany, and had just returned home for the first time in eight years after fighting in Palestine. Also in this picture are Maureen Nicholls, Billy Green, Jim and Irene Oscroft, Nancy Morley, Sally Marsh, Lily Wood, Beryl Bull, Betty Bull, Dot Bull, Barbara Bull, Pam Copestake, Muriel Copestake, Maggie Collier, Mrs Warriner, Franklin Warriner, Daisy Wood, Tony Wood, Billy Wood and Alan Quemby. Devonshire Street, which adjoined Station Road, was one of the five central Shirebrook streets demolished in the 1970s.